To Josh,
Merry Christmas 2007
Rob, Sandi, and Jesse

The Alaska We Love

The Alaska We Love

Blue Skies Above Texas Company
Memorial Drive #399
Houston, TX 77079

All rights reserved. No part of this book may be reproduced or transmitted by any means, electronic or mechanical, including photocopying, recording, or by any information storage and retrieval system, without written permission from the authors, except for the inclusion of brief quotations in a review.

Copyright © 2007 by Blue Skies Above Texas Company

Edition ISBN
978-0-9800019-0-7

Text, Captions, and Photography by
Sandra Stone
James Stone
B. G. (Rob) Irby

Acknowledgement

We would like to express our gratitude to the amazing people of Alaska who made preparing this book such a pleasurable experience. The state is truly the "Last Frontier" and the people are strong asset. There was not a single location that we did not find the people friendly and helpful.

The Alaska Range – The natural beauty of Alaska.

Roads lead into the last frontier and new adventure.

Anchorage

Approximately 42% of Alaska's population lives in an area of about 1955 square miles making Anchorage about the size of the State of Delaware. This is a modern city surrounded by spectacular wilderness. Although not incorporated until 1920, the city was established by Captain James Cook on his third voyage in 1778 but took hold with the building of the Alaska Railroad.

A statue of Captain James Cook stands overlooking Cook Inlet

CAPTAIN JAMES COOK

R.N., F.R.S.

Navigator, Explorer, Chartmaker, Scientist, Humanist

1728-1779

James Cook was born in Yorkshire, England, on October 27, 1728. He was apprenticed to serve on sailing ships built in Whitby, near his birth-place, to carry coal along the English coast. At age 26, he joined the Royal Navy, took part in actions against France and, through his natural flair for mathematics and science, was promoted "King's Surveyor" and given command of vessels performing survey work on the coast of Newfoundland. Chosen as commander to lead an expedition of discovery to the Pacific Ocean, he sailed on his first voyage of exploration (1768-71) to find the continent of Australia as well as Tahiti, New Zealand and New Guinea where he charted coasts and waters previously unknown to the Western World. On his return, he was honored by a grateful nation, made a Fellow of the Royal Society, and received by the King.

His second voyage (1772-75) to Antarctic and the South Pacific added the Friendly Isles, New Caledonia, Easter Island, Cook Island and New Georgia to the map.

In 1776, Captain Cook set out on his third voyage, aboard his flagship "Resolution", to find a north-west passage from the Pacific to the Atlantic. He surveyed the coast of northwest America and Alaska, but, failing to find the passage to the Atlantic, turned south from the Bering Strait and sailed to the Sandwich Isles where, on the Island of Hawaii, he met his death on February 14, 1779.

James Cook, a farm hand's son who became a Captain in the Royal Navy and gold medalist of the Royal Society, lives in history as the greatest explorer-navigator the world has known. His real memorial is on the map of the world.

This monument, created by Derek Freeborn after the statue in Whitby, where James Cook began his career as a seaman, was donated by The British Petroleum Company as a contribution to the Bicentennial celebration of the United States of America.

This is a bear and raven statue in the tourist section downtown Anchorage with a plaque giving the following inscription:

Ice fishing adventure on Jewel Lake is an annual event in Anchorage. The lake covers 28 acres and is stocked with rainbow trout, Chinook salmon, and artic char.

The Moose even wander through Anchorage in search of food. It is against the law to feed wildlife in Alaska but the animals are resourceful and well able to take care of themselves. This one is easily recognizable since he has one antler missing. He is grazing on berries only a few feet from an office building in Midtown Anchorage. Some 800 moose live in greater Anchorage.

The trees in winter here look like the flocked trees that are present during the Christmas season in the lower forty-eight. The difference here is that the decoration is by nature.

From Anchorage, six mountain ranges can be seen. These are Chugach, Kenai, Takleetna, Tordrillo, Aleutian, and Alaska. The beauty is breath taking.

The sunset as seen from a vantage point on the hillside east of Anchorage gives one the sense of the beauty and peacefulness of this wilderness.

On the opposite page are scenes of the beautiful mountains that are ever present.

Across the Cook Inlet sits the mountain Susitna referred to as "Sleeping Lady". The native legend is that her lover was killed and her friends could not bear to tell her. Rather than waking her, they asked the gods to protect her until peace returned to the land. The gods complied and now she sleeps under a blanket of green grass in summer and soft snow in winter.

View of Anchorage from Point Mackenzie across the Cook Inlet. The area was named for the Rt. Hon. James Stuart MacKenzie in 1794. It was a supply center for mining. The area was essentially abandoned when the Alaska railroad bypassed it in 1917.

Seward Highway

South of Anchorage on the Seward highway, we see our national and state flag flying with Turnagain Arm in the background.

On the highway from Anchorage to Seward, there is an old iron horse parked. This railroad snow clearing engine, created by Orange Jull in 1883, was used to clear the tracks to keep the trains running all winter. This equipment would literally throw snow hundreds of feet from the track. They are rarely used now as the Caterpillar D-6s are more efficient.

The sunlight through the trees gives this public campsite a heavenly glow and a peaceful appeal.

There are footpaths to be found all over with spectacular views. The foot and cycle paths range from easy to difficult.

In the spring water falls can be seen draining melting snow down the mountain sides.

The view of the mountains and Turnagain Arm of the Cook Inlet is a sight to remember.

South of Anchorage is the town of Girdwood. A favorite ski resort is Alyeska.

This view of the resort is from the top of the tram lift. It is a spectacular seven minute ride to the top of Mt. Alyeska. At the top there is a panoramic view of majestic mountains, hanging glaciers, streams, towering spruce, and a vantage point to observe different wildlife.

The Crow Creek Mine is located near Girdwood. Active claims still sprinkle the stream. This is an old vehicle parked near the entrance of the mining area which is now a tourist attraction with old buildings and the opportunity to pan for gold.

A house beside the highway is a reminder that the area is an earthquake zone. This house was rendered uninhabitable by a major quake in 1964. This March 27, 1964 earthquake was the second largest of the twentieth century and the largest recorded in the northern hemisphere. A 9.2 magnitude triggered a west coast destructive tsunami.

This would be quite a "fixer-upper",

The view from the opposite side of Turnagain Arm on the way to Hope is as spectacular as from the highway to Seward.

Hope is an old mining town. It is now a town with great attractions for fishing, camping and of course, photography.

Exit Glacier is located in the Kenai Fjords National Park near Seward. The park covers 917 square miles or about 587,000 acres of the Kenai Peninsula. There are paths to see and explore the glacier.

Seward

St. Peters Episcopal Church

The harbor at Seward is the home of many pleasure and fishing craft as well as many tour boats.

The Bald Eagle overlooking the harbor is ever vigilant for food.

A sailboat on Resurrection Bay is seen from Seward. The town was named for William H. Seward, one of the people responsible for the territory's purchase from Russia in 1867. Seward was founded in 1903 by the Alaska Railroad surveyors. It was the starting place for miners and suppliers going to interior gold fields via the Iditarod Trail.

Mountains rising from Resurrection Bay are near Seward. An interesting fact is how this bay got its' name. It was named by Alexander Baranov, who because of a bad storm in the Gulf of Alaska had to retreat to the bay. By the time the storm settled, it was Easter Sunday. So, the bay and the nearby river were named Resurrection.

North

The town of Talkeetna is some 115 miles north of Anchorage. In the summer, Talkeetna offers fishing and air tours of Denali Park. Talkeetna is also used as a base for climbers embarking on the challenge of climbing Mount McKinley.

The remains of the old Independence Mine, near Hatchers Pass, are now a State Park. Gold was discovered in the area. The gold found in the bottom of pans and sluice boxes indicated that there must be a nearby source or mother lode. The elaborate tunnels and heavy equipment required are expensive. Companies merged to pool resources. At its peak in 1941 there were over 200 men employed at the mine.

The skies over Alaska on a cool crisp evening in late November. The sun is setting on the horizon and the moon is seen over the landscape.

A war memorial is on the Parks highway near the Denali National Park. The area is clearly marked.

Winter scenes near Denali National Park.

Majestic mountains are everywhere.

The tallest mountain in North America is Mount McKinley or Denali.

This mountain can be seen on the horizon from miles and miles away.

This view is of the Alaska Range from the Denali Highway. This 135 mile stretch of road runs between Cantwell and Paxson linking the Richardson and Parks highways. The road is paved for about 20 miles on each end with the remainder maintained only during the summer. Wildlife is abundant.

These trees have been naturally flocked by Mother Nature. The temperature is a chilly 30 degrees below zero Fahrenheit in Healy.

Transportation

Alaska Railroad

Building of the Alaska Railroad began in 1902 from Seward. The railroad was taken over by the federal government and was officially finished in 1923 when President Warren G. Harding tapped a golden spike. In 1985, the State of Alaska bought the railroad from the US government.

Trans-Alaska Pipeline

Crude oil from the North Slope is transported via the 800 mile long Trans Alaska Pipeline originating from Prudhoe Bay through the rugged and beautiful Alaska terrain to America's northernmost ice-free port at Valdez.

The 48-inch pipeline is like a long silver snake on the ground. The pipeline passes over three mountain ranges and crosses 800 rivers and streams. It was constructed to resist earth quakes, gun shots, and not to interfere with caribou and moose migration paths. This $8 billion construction started in 1975. First oil flowed in June of 1977.

There are other forms of transportation such as air and water which are not included here.

Wildlife

Bald Eagle

The bald eagle is not really bald. Bald used to mean white. About half of the 70,000 eagles in North America nest in Alaska. They feed on salmon as well as other food sources.

Mallard Ducks

Did these birds arrive too early?

A whole flock landed looking for Spring.

A favorite photo is of this Mallard.

Some pose and show off. The water is cold and this bird is late in leaving.

Raven

There are many ravens in the south of Alaska. The common raven grows to 22 to 27 inches and weighs 1.5 to 3.6 pounds. They coexist with humans and feed on insects and food waste, in addition to cereal grains, berries, fruit and small animals.

Magpie

One of the more common and conspicuous birds is the Black-Billed Magpie. This is a colorful bird which many look on as a nuisance. Unlike most birds, this jay can locate food by scent.

Swans

Among the more beautiful and elegant birds are the swans. There are three species in Alaska. These, we believe are the Trumpeter Swans. They were located at Potter's Marsh.

Grebe

There are many rivers and lakes. Birds may stop briefly or may nest. One unusual species is the Grebe. This bird has lobed toes and is normally seen on land or water more often than in the air. These were found on Mirror Lake just north of Anchorage.

Canadian Geese

Canadian Geese are among the many nesting birds which come to Potter's Marsh near Anchorage.

The white chinstrap on the black head and neck distinguish this goose from all others, but the Barnacle Goose. These elegant birds mate for life unless one of them is killed.

Ptarmigan

Throughout the year there are birds everywhere. These include the state bird, the Ptarmigan. The migration range of this bird keeps it mostly within the state.

This is the spring and summer attire. The birds are quite tame and approachable for close range snap shots.

This ptarmigan is in transition from winter to summer plumage.

A playful sea otter floats lazily on the surface of the water. Many animals can be seen on the organized tours out of Seward.

There are a few Steller or Northern Sea Lions relaxing on a rock. They get their name because they resemble the African lion. The large adult males appear to have a mane due to long coarse hair on large necks and shoulders. Fully grown males are about 10 feet long and weigh about 1250 pounds while the smaller females measure almost 9 feet and weigh 580 pounds.

It takes a sharp eye to spot some of the wildlife such as this Red Squirrel nestled in a tree nibbling on a snack. These rodents store these spruce cones in a hiding place measuring 15 to 18 foot by 3 foot. They are territorial with a ½ to 1 acre range.

The Snowshoe hare here in Denali National Park looks like a cuddly stuffed animal. The hares' back feet are so big it looks like it is wearing big shoes so it won't sink into the snow. Thus, how it got its name. Denali means "the high one" translated from Athabascan. Denali National Park is as big as Vermont and the oldest national park in Alaska.

The wildlife is varies and unique. Dall Sheep are abundant and interesting. There are 50,000 in Alaska; however, they are not often seen. One viewing place is on the cliffs above Seward Highway which is a birthing place.

There is a variety of wildlife to be seen and enjoyed in this unique wonderland. The muskoxen are at home in the harsh climate.

The Inupiat Eskimos called the arctic ground squirrel "tsik-tsik" because of the sound it makes when alarmed.

The female alpha wolf of a healthy grey wolf pack resident in Denali National Park, she is a good mother to her five pups. The pups will leave the pack at two or three years old and will find a mate for life. Then they start their own pack.

The wolf packs range from 2 to 15 with 4 to 7 being family members and relatives. The leader is usually the strongest male. He is the alpha male and dominant over the whole pack. Where as the alpha female may only be dominant over some of the lower-ranking males.

This Brown Bear may look like a huggable teddy bear but he is a wild animal and can be dangerous. Bears found in coastal areas where salmon is the primary food source are referred to as "brown bears" while "brown bears" found inland and in northern habitats are often called "grizzlies". Technically, both are the same. The fur can be light blonde to dark brown.

Caribou herds roam the countryside near Denali Park.

One finds all sorts of animals up in trees. This porcupine is resting.

The Anchorage Moose

The abundance of plants to graze on helps the moose to survive during the long winter months.

Occasionally a stray moose finds warmth and substance from the garbage around apartments and houses in the city.

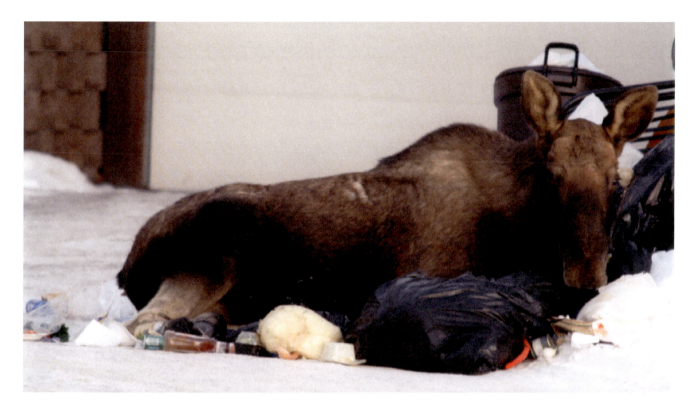

You might even think that this moose likes it well enough here to buy the condominium advertised, or perhaps the sign might be an attractive snack.

The sign must not have been satisfying, so this moose switches to twigs. A 1000 pound adult cow moose will consume 10 pounds of frozen plant matter daily.

This one is curious to see those silly humans on display.

Looking over the railing at the edge of the patio, she does not understand why she cannot coerce a snack.

Guess it is time to go on.

Bye for now.